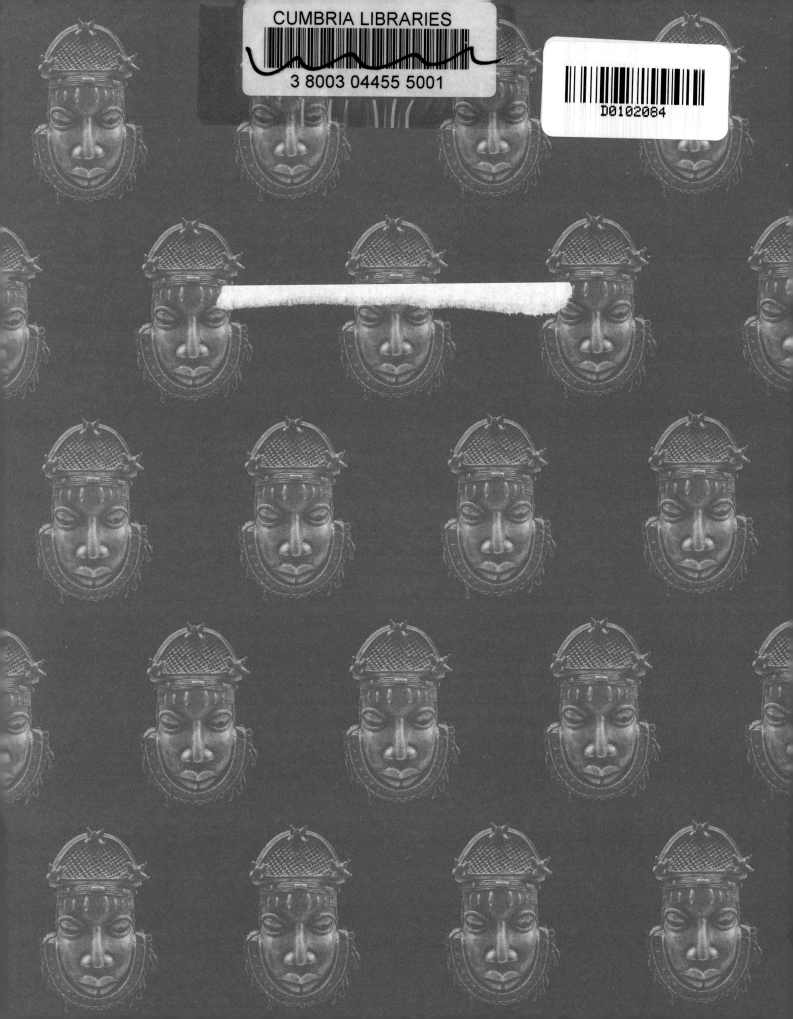

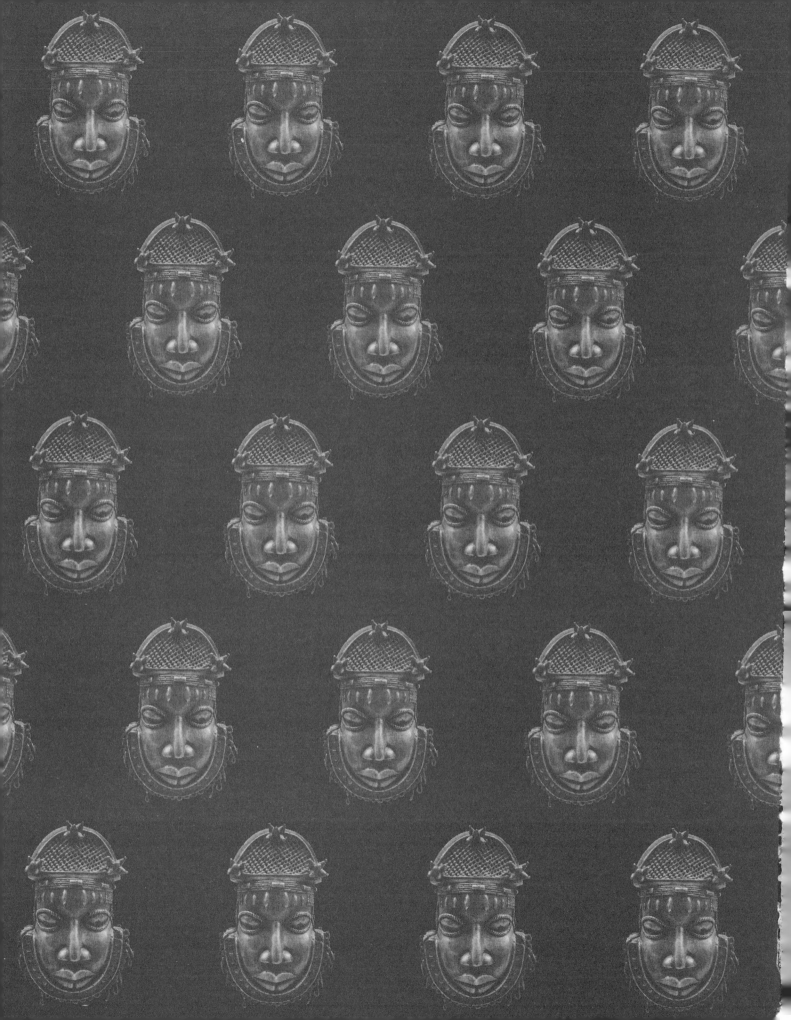

BENIN
900–1897CE

THE HISTORY DETECTIVE INVESTIGATES

Alice Harman

WAYLAND

First published in 2014 by Wayland

Copyright © Wayland 2014

Wayland
338 Euston Road
London NW1 3BH

Wayland Australia
Level 17/207 Kent Street
Sydney, NSW 2000

The History Detective Investigates series:

Produced for Wayland by
White-Thomson Publishing Ltd
www.wtpub.co.uk
+44 (0)843 208 7460

Editor: Alice Harman
Designer: Alix Wood
Cover design concept: Lisa Peacock
Consultant: Philip Parker
Proofreader: Lucy Ross

A catalogue record for this title is available from the British Library.

ISBN: 978-0-7502-8178-2
eBook ISBN: 978-0-7502-8563-6

Dewey Number: 966.8'301-dc23

Printed in Malaysia

10 9 8 7 6 5 4 3 2 1

Wayland is a division of Hachette Children's Books, an Hachette UK company

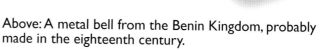

Above: A metal bell from the Benin Kingdom, probably made in the eighteenth century.

Previous page: This sixteenth-century mask is one of the most famous artworks from the Benin Kingdom.

Cover top: This arm ornament is in the shape of a leopard. It was part of an outfit worn by a Benin king for special ceremonies.

Cover bottom: Benin's royal palace was decorated with many metal plaques like this one. The king is shown here on horseback, supported by two soldiers.

CONTENTS

Words in **bold** can be found in the glossary on page 30.

The history detective Sherlock Bones will help you to find clues and collect evidence about the Benin. Wherever you see one of Sherlock's paw-prints, you will find a mystery to solve. The answers are on page 31.

WHERE WAS BENIN?

Today, there is a country in West Africa that is called Benin. It is named after a great civilization that existed from 900–1897 CE, in an area of West Africa further to the east. This civilization is known as the Benin Kingdom. People sometimes also call it the Benin Empire.

The Benin Kingdom occupied an area of land that stretched back from the West African coast. This area is now in south-west Nigeria. The capital of the kingdom was Benin City, and there is still a city of that name on the same site. However, the city was destroyed by British forces in 1897 and only parts of the old city walls and **moats** remain today.

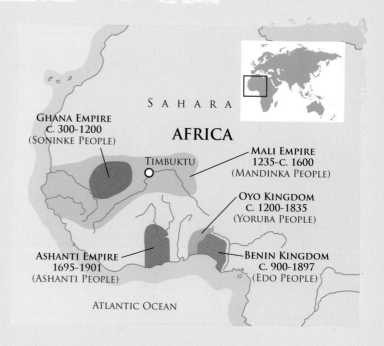

This map shows the Benin Kingdom and some of the other kingdoms that existed in West Africa at the time.

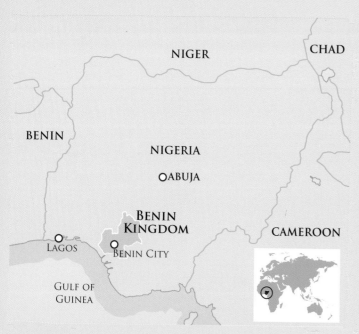

This map shows part of West Africa today. The Benin Kingdom came to an end in 1897, but in present-day Nigeria there is still an area called the Benin Kingdom. Its capital is Benin City.

🐾 **Today, in which country can the remains of ancient Benin City's walls and moats be found?**

Benin was near to other powerful civilizations, such as the Oyo Kingdom, as well as many smaller **settlements**. It also had access to overland trade routes across Africa, which ran to and from the great city of Timbuktu. Benin's position on the coast meant that it had a lot of contact with traders who travelled across the ocean from Europe.

Benin's location linked it to several different cultures, such as the Ashanti Empire and the Mali Empire, and the kingdom was influenced by them throughout its 1,000-year existence. Although Benin had a strong traditional identity, it also included elements of other cultures to help it grow into a wealthy and highly developed civilization.

The borders of the Benin Kingdom changed frequently and no records were kept of these changes, so it is unclear exactly how large it was. However, it was definitely not the largest of the West African civilizations. Historians agree that the Mali Empire, to the north-west, was much bigger.

Benin produced many beautiful works of art. It is particularly famous for its metal artworks, which were made by very skillful craftsmen.

DETECTIVE WORK

Visit www.metmuseum.org/toah/hd/beni_2/hd_beni_2.htm to learn about the traditional shared history of the Benin Kingdom and the neighbouring city-states of Owo and Ijebu.

In a study called 'Benin: An African Kingdom', historians from the British Museum wrote:

'Until the late 19th century, one of the major powers in West Africa was the kingdom of Benin in what is now southwest Nigeria.'

WHO WERE THE FIRST PEOPLE OF BENIN?

The first people of Benin were the Edo people, an ethnic group of West Africans who speak the Edo language. Edo people made up most of Benin's population throughout its existence, although as the kingdom grew it took in some people from other states and ethnic groups.

There are no written records to document Benin's early history, so historians have to use **archaeological** evidence and stories passed down to later generations to put together theories about its origins. Many of the stories are traditional, **mythical** ones that involve magic and gods, and it can be difficult to find any facts within them.

Encyclopaedia Britannica gives details about how many Edo people there are today, and where they live:

'The Edo numbered about 3.8 million at the turn of the 21st century. Their territory is west of the Niger River and extends from hilly country in the north to swamps in the Niger Delta.'

This Edo boy is a descendant of the people of the Benin Kingdom. Many Edo people live in the Benin Kingdom area of Nigeria today. They call this area Edo.

From around 900 CE the first people of Benin lived in small neighbouring communities that together formed a kingdom. This kingdom was ruled by a single king and was protected by a network of earth walls and moats. There is archaeological evidence of this early kingdom: a large network of walls and moats have been found in the area around modern Benin City, and they are believed to have been built from 900 CE to 1400 CE.

This early civilization was known as Igodomigodo until around 1180 CE, when its name was changed to Edo. It was only when Portuguese people arrived in the area in the late fifteenth century that the name Benin started to be used, but this name is now widely used to describe the entire civilization from 900–1897 CE.

This mask was made in Benin in the eighteenth century. It was used in the Ododua ceremony, which celebrates the founding of the Benin Kingdom.

This is one small remaining section of an earth wall around Benin City.

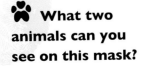

🐾 **What two animals can you see on this mask?**

WHO WERE THE LEADERS OF BENIN?

From 900–1180 CE, when early Benin was known as Igodomigodo, it was ruled by a mysterious dynasty of kings called Ogisos. There is very little information about the dynasty, but it is believed that up to thirty-one kings ruled during this time. The Edo word 'Ogiso' means 'King of the Sky'. In traditional stories, Ogisos lived in a timeless and partly mythical world and they helped to create Edo society.

🐾 Does the word 'Oba' originally come from the Edo language?

Around 1180 CE, although the dates are not exact in this early era of Benin's history, a new dynasty began with a ruler named Eweka I. He is said to have been an Ogiso descendant, living in the neighbouring area of Yorubaland, who was invited to take over the kingdom. He took the title of Oba, which means 'king' in the Yoruba language, and all rulers of Benin from this point on were known by this title. He also changed the kingdom's name from Igodomigodo to Edo.

From 1440 CE onwards, Benin grew from a thriving city-state into a great, wealthy kingdom. There is more written evidence of Benin's leaders during this time. An Oba known as Ewuare the Great took over Benin in about 1440 CE, following a period of **civil war** against his brother. Ewuare's son and grandson continued his work enlarging the Benin Kingdom.

This is a sculpture of an Oba's head. The strings of precious coral beads around the Oba's neck show his wealth and status.

DETECTIVE WORK

Although Obas were always men, women in the royal family did have power and influence. Find out about Idia, a famous 'Queen Mother' of Benin: www.metmuseum.org/toah/hd/pwmn_3/hd_pwmn_3.htm

Many chiefs helped the Oba to run Benin, although the Oba still held absolute power. The Uzama was a group of important chiefs who traditionally chose Benin's Obas. However, Ewuare's grandson – Oba Esigie – limited the Uzama's power during his reign and the group lost a lot of its influence from then on.

The Oba was the head of the military, and approved plans for the army's movements and tactics. The strict organization of Benin's military missions was part of the reason for their success. Merchants could only trade with the Oba's permission, and he was in charge of trading the most expensive goods, such as **ivory** and slaves.

Obas were all-powerful and highly respected in Benin, and much of the kingdom's art was made to honour these kings and their families. The art was often displayed in the Obas' grand palaces. The Oba was seen as semi-**divine** because people thought he could communicate with the worlds of gods and spirits.

In this nineteenth-century print, the Oba is shown parading through Benin, accompanied by musicians and a pair of leopards used for special ceremonies.

The respected **curator** Joseph Eboreime has said that metal plaques were created for these reasons:

'To commemorate significant historical events.

To glorify the Oba (King) as well as the awe and the glamour of kingship.

[To illustrate] shared religious beliefs, myths and traditions.'

This metal plaque shows Oba Orhogbua, who ruled Benin for around thirty years during the sixteenth century.

WHEN WAS BENIN'S GOLDEN AGE?

There is not much written evidence of Benin's development before Portuguese traders arrived in the kingdom in the late fifteenth century. This is because the Edo people traditionally passed on history by speaking it aloud rather than writing it down.

However, it is known that by the fifteenth century Benin had become an important power in the West African region. This was partly because the kingdom was ideally situated for trade. It linked the West African coast with the trade routes that crossed the Sahara desert further inland. This trade made Benin rich, and the money was used to develop the kingdom.

The historian Kevin Shillington has said:

'Apparently one of the keys to Benin's wealth was its location at a junction of east-west and north-south trade.'

This meant that the kingdom could make money by selling on goods from elsewhere to the Europeans.

Benin's continued growth and development eventually led to the Golden Age of Benin. This is what historians call a period of time in the fifteenth and sixteeth centuries during which Benin controlled a considerable area of land in the region and was at the height of its power and wealth. Many of the kingdom's most beautiful works were made in this period, including most of its famous metal plaques.

This ivory mask shows Idia, a powerful female member of Benin's royal family at the end of the fifteenth century.

What was Idia's royal title?

Oba Ewuare was Benin's first Golden Age ruler, and he conquered many neighbouring towns and villages during his reign. His son, Ozolua, further expanded the Benin Kingdom by leading aggressive military campaigns and winning 200 battles. On pages 20–21, there is more information about Benin's famously strong army.

In 1514 Ozolua's son, Oba Esigie, set up trading agreements to formalise arrangements with merchants who had travelled from Portugal. Other European visitors came after the Portuguese, with the first English traders arriving in Benin in 1553. Trade with Europeans as well as African states brought in great wealth for the kingdom.

Europeans also supplied Benin with guns and served as **mercenaries** in the kingdom's armies, which allowed Benin to expand more rapidly and successfully. Captives from campaigns into neighbouring territories were often sold as slaves to the Portuguese traders, which created more wealth for Benin.

DETECTIVE WORK
Look in detail at a piece of art showing the Oba with Portuguese traders, and listen to a podcast about its history: www.bbc.co.uk/ ahistoryoftheworld/objects/ rmAT6B7zTZCGACd7i7l6Wg

This plaque shows a chief in full battle dress, with his attendants surrounding him. Benin's strong army helped to enlarge the kingdom during its Golden Age.

WHAT DID BENIN CITY LOOK LIKE?

Much of what we know about Benin City is based on accounts given by European visitors to Benin, from the fifteenth century onwards. They were all impressed by the size, organization and splendour of the city, and by the Oba and his **court**.

A Portuguese captain said that Benin City was a wealthy, productive place where there was no theft and people often did not have doors on their houses. Spanish visitors apparently got lost in the grand complex of palace buildings, and had great difficulty finding any of the **officials** that they wanted to meet there.

The Dutch writer Olfert Dapper compiled a detailed description of Benin City in 1668. This account was based on reports from European travellers, however, as he had not visited the city himself. Dapper describes a large and spacious city built along wide, straight roads. He mentions the many great palaces, houses and apartments for the Oba and his court, which were built around square courtyards and decorated with metal plaques.

DETECTIVE WORK

In Sheet 3 of the worksheets, at the link below, read some more European accounts of what Benin City looked like. Notice how the figures relating to the Benin Walls are different to those mentioned in the quote on this page; you will find that historians often do not agree on facts and interpretations: www.britishmuseum.org/pdf/KingdomOfBenin_StudentsWorksheets.pdf

This drawing of Benin City was published in Dapper's 1668 *Description of Benin*. Historians are not sure that the city actually looked like this, as the drawing was created by someone who had heard visitors' accounts but hadn't seen the city.

🐾 **What two musical instruments can you see people playing in the parade?**

The European visitors noted that there was a huge network of earth walls around the city and its surrounding lands. These walls were called *iya*, and in places they were up to 20 m (66 ft) high. Parts of the walls still exist, although they are being destroyed despite people's efforts to protect them. The earth walls helped to defend Benin from invaders as well as defining the boundaries of different settlements. They seem to have provided an effective defence, as rival powers such as the Oyo Kingdom and the Igala Kingdom both apparently tried and failed to conquer Benin City.

Science writer Fred Pearce wrote in *New Scientist* magazine about the enormous length of the Benin Walls:

'The [Benin Walls] extend for some 16,000 kilometres in all… They cover 6,500 square kilometres and were all dug by the Edo people. In all, they are four times longer than the Great Wall of China, and consumed a hundred times more material than the Great Pyramid of Cheops. They took an estimated 150 million hours of digging to construct.'

This plaque shows the entrance to the Oba's palace. The two pillars at the entrance have the faces of Portuguese traders on them. This is because trade with Europe was so important to the kingdom's wealth and power.

Throughout Benin's existence, civil wars brought unrest and destruction to Benin City. In the late seventeenth century, after one civil war, a Dutch merchant named David van Nyendael described the city as **desolate** and empty of people. Continual fighting had reduced the population, and large parts of the city were apparently left deserted and crumbling into ruins.

However, Benin City seems to have recovered well after periods of civil war, and the city was eventually rebuilt to its former glory. The English explorer Sir Richard Burton visited in 1862 and described the city's large, handsome houses built with clay walls, and its long, broad streets where permanent markets were held.

WHAT WAS LIFE LIKE FOR ORDINARY PEOPLE IN BENIN?

Not very much is known about the ordinary people of Benin because most of the historical evidence we have is from the kingdom's art and the European visitors' accounts. These almost always focus on the rich and powerful people of Benin. Ordinary people and their normal, modest living conditions are hardly featured at all.

The lives of ordinary citizens, including highly skilled craftspeople, were not recorded in Benin's art. However, we can see the extraordinary talent of these craftsmen in the art that they created.

Many people were farmers, working hard to clear the forest and plant vegetables, often yams. However, people could not own the land on which they lived and farmed or worked. All land was **communal** and was held by the Oba. People usually lived in large families, as they were encouraged to have several children to make sure there were many people to work the land.

🐾 Are the people shown in Benin's plaques ordinary farmers and craftspeople?

In Benin City, many craftsmen worked with metal, wood and ivory. Lots of them worked for the Oba. There were **guilds** of craftsmen, and these workers lived in a special area of the city. Pottery was also made in the city, and it was probably women rather than men who created it.

Other people in Benin were very skilled at making mud buildings, and ordinary people would probably have lived comfortably in these homes. The buildings were sometimes decorated with polished red walls with horizontal lines cut into them.

Benin had many traditional festivals throughout the year, and people would take part in celebrations or rituals for these occasions. The Igue festival was one of the Benin Kingdom's most important events, and it took place in the last days of the year. It is believed to have originally celebrated Oba Ewuare's marriage to his wife Ewere, and its purpose was to renew the Oba's magical powers. The Igue festival is still celebrated in Nigeria today.

The British Museum gives more information on the guilds of Benin, to which many people in Benin City belonged:

'The guild of blacksmiths and ironsmiths supplied the weapons of war and other implements, while the guild of bronze-casters and carvers supplied all objects required by the palace. Also practising were the guilds of doctors, leather-workers, drummers, leopard hunters, dancers and carpenters.'

DETECTIVE WORK

Find out about the ceremonies and festivals of Benin by clicking on each of the last five tabs in the list – you can also find out more about farming and food at the 'Agriculture' tab: eachi.org/history.html

Benin women created everyday ceramic objects, such as pots, but men made ceremonial ceramic artworks.

WHAT GOODS DID BENIN TRADE WITH EUROPE?

Until the middle of the seventeenth century, Benin mostly sold European traders goods such as peppers, ivory, cloth, leopard skins, beads, rubber, palm oil and precious stones. Many of these goods were bought further inland and then sold on to the Europeans for a higher price, rather than being produced inside Benin.

In return, Benin bought a lot of metal from Europeans, and used much of it to create the metalwork art for which the kingdom is famous. It doesn't seem as though Benin's art was sold on in Europe, although we know some artworks were created for Portuguese traders. Artworks stolen from Benin in the 1890s are described as the first of their kind seen in Europe. Benin also bought luxury items from the Europeans, such as fine textiles and coral that was made into jewellery. Later, alcoholic spirits, tobacco and guns were also popular **imports**.

Benin was keen to buy guns from the Portuguese early on in their trading relationship, and some people from Benin travelled to Portugal in 1514 to request permission to do so. However, the Portuguese did not want to sell them to Benin. This was partly because Benin was not a Christian kingdom, and partly because Benin refused to sell male slaves to Portugal. By the seventeenth century, however, Benin managed to buy guns from European traders.

Can you tell what is shown at the top of the salt cellar?

This finely carved ivory salt cellar shows Portuguese noblemen around the base and a European ship on the upper part. These and similar ivory objects were made by Benin craftsmen for the Portuguese traders.

DETECTIVE WORK

Find out more about the goods that were traded between Europe and Africa at www.metmuseum.org/toah/hd/aftr/hd_aftr.htm

This Portuguese man is holding a matchlock, a type of gun that traders carried and sold to Benin. He is shown here using the gun for hunting rather than fighting.

By the mid-seventeenth century, slaves had become Benin's most profitable **export**. At first, Benin only sold women as slaves. The kingdom's powerful army made raids on neighbouring territories, and female captives were sold to the Europeans. Women were also sometimes bought from neighbouring communities, and Benin made a profit by selling them on as slaves. From the mid-seventeenth century, however, the slave trade was so important to Benin that male captives and even the kingdom's own citizens were sold into slavery.

At the height of its slave trade, Benin sold 3,000 people a year to the Europeans. The trade continued into the late nineteenth century, although by this time it had been banned in some European countries and so Benin did not make as much money from it.

This sixteenth-century brass statue shows an Oba wearing head and neck pieces made of coral beads. Only the Oba was allowed to own coral items, but he shared them with people in his royal court.

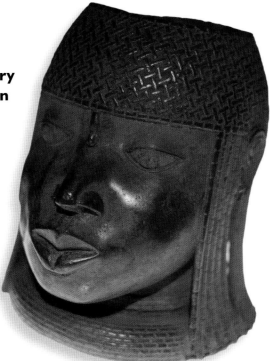

Historian Dmitri Bondarenko explains that the wealth of the Benin Kingdom was not only due to the slave trade:

'The rise of Benin... began several decades before the Europeans' arrival and ended in the early 17th century, long before the slave trade's end.'

WHY WERE ANIMALS IMPORTANT IN BENIN'S ART?

In Benin's art, the meaning of various animals is often linked to myths and traditional beliefs. Animals were important in Benin for this reason, and images of them appear on plaques and jewellery and as sculptures.

Leopards were seen as powerful and important, the animal **counterpart** of the Oba. The leopard was known as the 'king of the Bush' just as the Oba was king of Benin. The Oba kept leopards for use in ceremonial parades and occasionally to provide a great sacrifice to the gods.

The crocodile and the python were associated with the water god Olokun, and in royal art they symbolize the Oba's link with the world of the gods. **Mudfish** were also often shown on plaques featuring the king, because they live in and out of water and this symbolizes the Oba's power over both land and sea — and over the kingdoms of humans, gods and spirits.

🐾 Which animals were linked to the water god Olokun?

This bronze armlet is a piece of jewellery that was worn around the upper arm. It features a crocodile head, complete with a mouth full of sharp teeth.

Historians from the British Museum explain why animals have special meaning when they appear in Benin's art:

'When we see various animals on plaques, they are there for more than just decoration. Throughout West Africa people tell stories and **proverbs** about all kinds of creatures, wild and domestic, and many of them have characters which reveal important human qualities, in these cases usually those of the king.'

The animals in Benin's art are linked to the 'ideal order' in which the people of Benin believed. In this order, the Oba was the dominant power on earth, with all other humans below him and then animals beneath them.

Animals such as chickens, cows, goats and mudfish, which did not pose great danger to humans and could easily be used for food, took their rightful place in the order by not challenging man's dominance. These animals were often sacrificed to the gods, and statues of them also seem to have been offered in place of the actual animal.

Dangerous animals such as the crocodile and the python, which did not take their rightful place beneath man in the 'ideal order', also often appear in Benin's art. They may have been included on plaques with images of the Oba to show the king's ability to dominate these rebellious creatures.

DETECTIVE WORK

Find out more about animals in Benin's art: www.prm.ox.ac.uk/ benin.html

This plaque shows the Oba's butchers sacrificing a cow. The people of Benin believed a cow was one of the animal sacrifices that most pleased the gods.

HOW STRONG WAS THE ARMY OF BENIN?

Benin's army was famously strong, and was one main reason why Benin became such a powerful force in its region. The army fought wars against neighbouring kingdoms, and also led conquests into surrounding territories to win land and capture slaves that they could sell on to the Europeans.

Benin's wealth meant that the army could use high-quality weapons made of strong materials. Before the seventeenth century, the Benin army mostly used brass and iron swords, wooden **crossbows**, long spears, and bows and poisoned arrows. When Portuguese traders arrived in the fifteenth century, they carried guns that had far more killing power than any of Benin's weapons.

Olfert Dapper wrote in 1668 about European visitors' reports of the Benin army's great strength:

'The King of Benin can in a single day make 20,000 men ready for war, and, if need be, 180,000, and because of this he has great influence among all the surrounding peoples.'

This small bronze statue, created around 1600 CE, shows a Portuguese soldier aiming a matchlock gun.

DETECTIVE WORK

Learn about a very unusual brass statue from Benin, which shows a warrior riding on the back of a giant snail: www.galerie-herrmann. com/arts/art3/lfe_ Benin/63_Schnecke/e_ Schnecke_Krieger.htm

Benin was not able to buy these guns, but some of the Portuguese men fought with guns as paid soldiers alongside Benin's army. This made the army much stronger than neighbouring armies that used traditional weapons. From the seventeenth century onwards, Benin was able to buy guns from European traders. Although the army only allowed senior officers to use them in battle, this was still enough to give Benin a massive advantage against others in the region.

The army wore tough protective clothing that also helped them in battle. Soldiers carried large shields made of wood, animal skin and **basketwork**. The chiefs and top warriors wore helmets, often made of wood and hard crocodile skin. They also had body armour, made of padded cloth and often covered with leopard skins, which stopped arrows and spears piercing the main part of the body. All this equipment gave the army an advantage in battle against poorer states or settlements that could not afford to equip their men so well.

The army also used musical instruments to scare their enemies before they started fighting. Each soldier wore a bell that he would ring as they went into battle, to frighten the opposing side. Other soldiers played large horns that added to the army's loud, threatening noise.

This plaque shows Benin warriors in battle, wearing protective clothing and carrying weapons.

Why did the Benin army play loud music as they went into battle?

WHAT WERE THE CAUSES OF BENIN'S DECLINE?

The Benin Kingdom declined after 1700 CE, and then recovered in the 1800s before being destroyed by the British at the end of the century. Not much is known about what went on in Benin during its period of decline. Civil wars in the late seventeenth century and early eighteenth century reduced its population and partly destroyed Benin City. The kingdom also seems to have lost much of its wealth as the European powers began to ban the slave trade and stop boats taking slaves from Africa.

Historians Paula Ben-Amos Girshick and John Thornton talk about the damage Benin suffered from civil war:

'Towards the end of the seventeenth century, a number of European observers noted that the Edo Kingdom of Benin had been racked for some years by civil war. One of the longest accounts, that of David van Nyendael, reported that as a result of this civil war, Benin City had been... reduced to a "mere village".'

One main reason for the civil wars was that people kept fighting about who should take over as Oba. There was also lots of unrest among ordinary people because they created wealth for the kingdom while the rich people did nothing but spend the money on themselves. Between the civil wars, Benin seems to have repaired damage and returned to normal activity quite quickly.

This early eighteenth-century metal hip pendant depicts a court official of Benin. Although this piece still shows a high level of skill, Benin has fewer artworks dating from this period of decline.

In the nineteenth century, Benin became wealthier again as international trade in textiles and palm oil developed. However, at this time European states were also trying to gain control of large territories in Africa. They could then make huge profits by taking the land's **resources** for free and selling their own country's goods to the people living there. This was known as the 'Scramble for Africa'.

The Oba became very worried about Europeans trying to take over Benin. He tried to stop contact with them by gradually stopping exports from Benin. Eventually, the kingdom only exported palm oil. Benin lost a lot of money, and the Europeans did not give up their aggressive plans.

DETECTIVE WORK

Read more about the motives behind the Scramble for Africa: www.bbc.co.uk/history/ british/abolition/scramble_ for_africa_article_01.shtml

These finely crafted ivory figures were produced during Benin's nineteenth-century revival. They are decorated with small discs of metal.

What animal are these figures supposed to be?

WHY WAS BENIN DESTROYED IN 1897?

By the end of the nineteenth century, Britain wanted to get hold of Benin's rubber resources. There was high demand for rubber because businesses in Europe needed tyres for bicycles and early motor cars. Britain could make much bigger profits if it didn't have to pay the people who owned the rubber trees. Britain said it wanted a closer trading relationship with Benin, but it actually wanted complete control of its resources and trade.

In 1892, Britain sent an official called Henry Galway (later changed to Gallwey) to Benin with a **treaty** for the Oba to sign. This demanded exclusive British control of all property and people in the Benin Kingdom. In return, it offered only the 'gracious favour and protection' of the British Empire.

Galway reported to Britain that Oba Ovonramwen had signed the treaty, but this is very unlikely. Firstly, the treaty was similar to others that the Oba had previously refused. Secondly, Ovonramwen was taking part in the Igue festival, and during this time the Oba is forbidden to have contact with any person from outside his kingdom.

Which of Benin's resources did the British particularly want to control?

Despite this, Britain acted as though Oba Ovonramwen had signed the treaty. In 1897, a small group of British officials travelled to Benin to enforce the treaty. They were unexpectedly met by Benin's troops near the kingdom, apparently because word had reached Benin that the men planned to take control of the kingdom. Several British officers were killed, and Britain called this event the 'Benin Massacre'.

This illustration of the 'Benin Massacre' was published in a French newspaper reporting the event in January 1897.

In response, Britain sent more than 1,200 soldiers to invade Benin and revenge the British deaths. This British invasion is known as the Punitive Expedition of 1897. The British troops destroyed Benin City, lighting fires that burned down a large part of the city. They **looted** the palaces and monuments, and took at least 2,500 – and possibly many more – pieces of Benin's artwork. Britain justified taking the artworks by saying that they would be used to cover the cost of arranging the Punitive Expedition.

After the invasion, Britain **exiled** Oba Ovonramwen to a place called Calabar, to the south-west of Benin City. Benin came under Britain's control and no longer existed as an independent kingdom. The area eventually became part of Nigeria, which became an independent country in 1960.

The British soldiers who destroyed Benin said that there was horrific violence and human sacrifice in the kingdom. However, they may very well have exaggerated or invented such details to try to justify Britain's actions. Historians at the Victoria and Albert Museum have said:

'In 1897... the British led a punitive raid on Benin City. Justification for this brutal event was sought, in the British press, by depicting the Oba and his people as "savages" who practised human sacrifice.'

DETECTIVE WORK

Read more about the aftermath of Benin's destruction: www.artic.edu/aic/collections/exhibitions/benin/conquest

This photograph was taken in 1897 during the Punitive Expedition. The three British soldiers are sitting in a destroyed section of the royal family's area of Benin City. Lying on the floor are many of Benin's metal plaques.

WHAT ARE THE BENIN BRONZES?

The Benin Bronzes are a collection of more than 900 metal plaques from Benin City. Some people think that there are actually more than 2,000 of these plaques. They originally decorated pillars in the Oba's royal palace, but British troops took most of them when they destroyed Benin City in 1897.

These looted plaques were sold to European museums and private collectors, and the money from the sales went to the British government. Today, most of the Benin Bronzes remain in museums across Europe and the USA, although some have now been bought back by Nigerian museums. A small number were never taken from Benin City by the British, and have stayed in the original area. Many people believe that because the Benin Bronzes were stolen by the British they should be returned to Nigeria. Others think that because the artworks were taken a long time ago they do not need to be given back now.

Although the plaques are known as 'bronzes', most of them are made of brass rather than bronze. The plaques were made in the sixteenth and seventeenth centuries by craftsmen in Benin City. Some of them depict the royal figures and court life of Benin, and others celebrate historical events and successful wars. They were designed to glorify the Oba and his achievements, and the king appears in ceremonial dress on many of the plaques.

The drummer shown on this brass plaque is playing two drums made of hollowed logs with long slits in them. The plaques were rectangular but many of them have been partly damaged and are incomplete today.

DETECTIVE WORK

Benin's metal plaques were made using a technique called 'cire perdue', which means 'lost wax' in French. Edo people in Nigeria still use this traditional method for metalwork today. Learn more about the 'cire perdue' technique: www.butterflybronze.com/Metal%20 Casting/The_Lost_Wax_Casting_ Process.php

When the British troops brought the plaques back from Benin in 1897, along with other artworks in ivory, ceramic and wood, they caused quite a stir. British people who had not visited Benin were shocked that a society they thought of as 'primitive' could produce such beautiful, sophisticated works.

At first, some people refused to believe that the artworks could have been made by African people. The Benin Bronzes and other examples of West African art became famous in Europe, and many artists and scholars began to appreciate their value. During the early 1900s, modern artists such as Pablo Picasso and Henri Matisse were heavily influenced by the style of artworks from Africa.

This plaque shows an Oba in ceremonial dress, carrying weapons. It is a particularly well-preserved example, with all parts still intact.

Nigerian poet and playwright Wole Soyinka talks about how important the Benin Bronzes are in understanding African history:

'When [you] see a Benin Bronze… it makes you understand that African society actually produced some great civilizations, established some great cultures. What happened to the Benin kingdom is a reminder of what happened in many, many other parts of the African continent.'

In 1897, did most people in Britain think that African cultures were as sophisticated as their own?

YOUR PROJECT

You now know about the development and fall of the Benin Kingdom, and about the beautiful artworks that this civilization created. Think carefully about what particularly interests you about Benin, and what you would like to study in depth. What will you choose to research and present from this great civilization?

You could draw your own design for a metal plaque in the style of the Benin Bronzes. Think about the subjects that these plaques often show, and look carefully at the style of the figures and at the background decoration.

You could also learn more about the Obas of the Benin Kingdom. Find as many names of Benin's Obas as you can, and order them by date in a timeline. Then you could use Internet resources and library books to find out about the Edo community in Nigeria today, and the role of the Oba in their society.

You could try making your own animal sculptures, like the ones that were created in the Benin Kingdom for sacrifices and ceremonies. Use modelling clay to mould these sculptures. Look at the images of animals in this book to see how artists in Benin showed them.

This image from 1964 shows the Oba at that time, Akenzua II, in ceremonial dress.

Alternatively, you could write two diary or blog entries, one set during Benin's Golden Age and the other just before the fall of Benin in 1897. These could be from the point of view of an Oba, a member of the royal court or an ordinary person living in Benin City.

Another idea might be to do more research into the slave trade at the time of the Benin Kingdom. Write a letter to the Oba of Benin to explain why he shouldn't sell people as slaves, even if it makes his kingdom rich. Or you could organize a class debate about whether Britain should have to return the Benin Bronzes, and other artworks, to Nigeria. Whichever side of the argument you choose to defend, you will have to do a lot of research to make a good case.

This bronze sculpture was created in the early sixteenth century, during Benin's Golden Age.

Project presentation

● Do plenty of research for your project. Use the Internet and your local or school library.

● If you are writing a diary or a blog entry for a person from the Benin Kingdom, imagine what questions you would ask them and what they might answer.

● Collect as many pictures as you can to illustrate your project. Print off images from the Internet or draw items that you see in museums.

● If you are organizing a debate, think about the questions that will you need to ask and answer. Try to think in advance about what points the other side might make, and to think of good responses to these points.

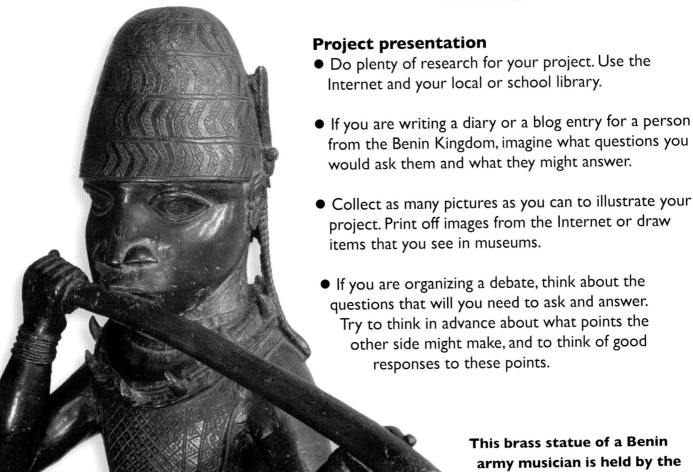

This brass statue of a Benin army musician is held by the British Museum.

GLOSSARY

archaeological Related to the remains of past civilizations.

basketwork Woven strips of natural material, such as leaves or bark.

brass A metal made up of two different metals, copper and zinc.

bronze A metal made up of two different metals, copper and tin.

CE 'Common Era'. Used to signify years since the believed birth of Jesus.

civil war A war between different sides in a state.

communal For use by every person in a group.

coral A hard, stony substance that is found on the ocean floor.

counterpart Something or someone that is like another object or person but in a different situation.

court The group of people who were close to the king.

crossbow A large, powerful type of bow.

curator Someone who organizes and presents objects in a museum or art gallery.

desolate Describes somewhere that seems empty, lonely and unhappy.

divine Related to gods.

dynasty A group of rulers from the same family.

exile To force someone to live in a different state and not allow them to return.

export Something a country sells to other countries.

guild An organization of people who all do the same job.

imports Goods that a country buys and brings in from other countries.

ivory Hard, pale-coloured material made from the teeth and tusks of animals.

loot To take objects from a place during a period of war or unrest.

mercenaries Soldiers who are paid to fight in another country's army.

moat A deep, wide ditch that surrounds a building or area and stops invaders.

mudfish A type of fish that can survive when there is little water by living in mud.

mythical Something related to a myth, which is a traditional story.

official A person who represents an organization or a state.

plaque A piece of hard material that is fixed to a wall or another surface and often written on or decorated.

proverb A short, well-known saying that expresses something true and wise.

resources Materials or other things that a person or group has and can use.

settlement A place where people live in a community.

salt cellar A container that holds salt.

treaty A formal agreement made between states.

ANSWERS

Page 4   The remains can be found in Nigeria.

Page 7   A crocodile and snake can be seen – they refer to dangerous spiritual forces that the king and other important figures control.

Page 8   No, it is originally a word from the Yoruba language.

Page 10   Idia was Queen Mother.

Page 12   People in the parade are playing drums and a tambourine.

Page 14   No, the people shown are usually Obas, other members of the royal family, chiefs, soldiers and Portuguese visitors.

Page 16   It is a ship. The head and hand of a Portuguese man are shown at the very top, poking out of the crow's nest of the ship. The crow's nest is the part of a ship from which people can look out into the distance.

Page 18   Crocodiles and snakes were linked to Olokun.

Page 21   The army played loud music to intimidate the other side before fighting began.

Page 23   They are sculptures of leopards. These figures stood at either side of the Oba's chair during special ceremonies.

Page 24   The British particularly wanted to control Benin's rubber resources.

Page 27   No, most British people at the time were shocked by the Benin Bronzes because they didn't think African cultures were advanced enough to create such great artworks.

FURTHER INFORMATION

Books to read

West African Kingdoms (Hands-on Ancient History) by Gary Barr (Heinemann 2007)

West African Kingdoms (Time Travel Guides) by John Haywood (Raintree 2007)

Discovering the Kingdom of Benin (Exploring African Civilizations) by Amie Jane Leavitt (Rosen 2014)

Websites

www.bbc.co.uk/schools/primaryhistory/worldhistory/benin_bronze/

kingdomofbenin.weebly.com

www.britishmuseum.org/PDF/british_museum_benin_art.pdf

www.prm.ox.ac.uk/benin.html

Note to parents and teachers: Every effort has been made by the publishers to ensure that these websites are suitable for children. However, because of the nature of the Internet, it is impossible to guarantee that the contents of these sites will not be altered. We strongly advise that Internet access is supervised by a responsible adult.

Places to visit
Pitt Rivers Museum, Oxford OX1 3PP
British Museum, London WC1B 3DG
World Museum, Liverpool L3 8EN

INDEX